ENERGY for LIFE

Energy from Fossil Fuels

Robert Snedden

Heinemann
LIBRARY

H www.heinemann.co.uk/library
Visit our website to find out more information about Heinemann Library books.

To order:
☎ Phone 44 (0) 1865 888066
▤ Send a fax to 44 (0) 1865 314091
▢ Visit the Heinemann Library Bookshop at www.heinemann.co.uk/library to browse our catalogue and order online.

First published in Great Britain by Heinemann Library,
Halley Court, Jordan Hill, Oxford OX2 8EJ
a division of Reed Educational and Professional Publishing Ltd.
Heinemann is a registered trademark of Reed Educational & Professional Publishing Ltd.

OXFORD MELBOURNE AUCKLAND
JOHANNESBURG BLANTYRE GABORONE
IBADAN PORTSMOUTH (NH) USA CHICAGO

© Reed Educational and Professional Publishing Ltd 2001
The moral right of the proprietor has been asserted.

Designed by Celia Floyd
Illustrated by Jeff Edwards and Alan Fraser
Originated by Ambassador Litho Ltd.
Printed in Hong Kong by Wing King Tong

ISBN 0 431 14642 X
06 05 04 03 02
10 9 8 7 6 5 4 3 2 1

British Library Cataloguing in Publication Data

Snedden, Robert
 Energy from fossil fuels. – (Energy for life)
 1. Fossil fuels
 I. Title
 333.8'2

Acknowledgements

The Publishers would like to thank the following for permission to reproduce photographs:
Austin J Brown/Aviation Picture Library: Pg.35; Camera Press: Pg.28, Pg.42; Corbis: Pg.4, Pg.9, Pg.18, Pg.19; Environmental Images: Pg.37, Pg.38, Pg.39; Hulton Deutsch: Pg.5; Hulton Getty: Pg.16, Pg.17; Mary Evans Picture Library: Pg.14, Pg.20, Pg.22; Paul Popper Ltd.: Pg.43; Robert Harding Picture Library: Pg.8, Pg.33; Science Photo Library: Pg.6, Pg.7, Pg.11, Pg.15, Pg.21, Pg.23, Pg.25, Pg.26, Pg.27, Pg.29, Pg.30, Pg.36, Pg.40, Pg.41; South American Pictures: Pg.13.

Cover photograph reproduced with permission of Photodisc.

Every effort has been made to contact copyright holders of any material reproduced in this book. Any omissions will be rectified in subsequent printings if notice is given to the Publisher.

Any words appearing in the text in bold, **like this**, are explained in the glossary.

Contents

Ancient sunlight

Energy makes things happen. In science, energy means the ability to do work. Any activity involves work because all activities involve energy. Even when you are asleep your body is at work, breaking down the food you eat, carrying out repairs and making new **cells**. A rock sitting motionless on the ground contains **chemical energy** in the bonds that hold its **atoms** together.

Life and energy

All life needs energy. Most of the energy used by life on Earth comes from the Sun. Green plants and some microbes can capture the Sun's energy and use it to make the food they need. The food that plants make for themselves in turn becomes the source of energy for all of the Earth's other organisms, which either eat plants or eat other animals that have eaten plants.

Without the Sun, the Earth would be a dark and lifeless rock.

People and energy

To begin with, people only had the strength of their own muscles to rely on. Later, the invention of agriculture provided another source of energy to draw on, as animals could be used to plough fields and transport goods. Mastering the use of fire allowed people to make pottery, forge metals and cook their food. Harnessing the energy of the wind to power sailing ships allowed people to travel along rivers and across seas.

This steam-powered locomotive makes use of the energy of the Sun stored in the coal it burns.

With the discovery of **fossil fuels** people found a new way of using the Sun's energy. Coal, **petroleum** and **natural gas** all contain energy from the Sun that was trapped by living plants and **micro-organisms** many millions of years ago. Fossil fuels, in particular coal, powered the **Industrial Revolution** that eventually led to today's high-technology society.

Today, we still rely on the ancient energy trapped in fossil fuels. We release the energy of petroleum in our aircraft and road vehicles. Natural gas heats homes and factories and is used to cook food. Coal, oil and gas are all used to provide the energy needed to generate electricity in power stations.

Energy supply

We use energy in different ways to provide light and heat, to operate machinery, to transport us from place to place and to make the things we need. The total of all of the energy we have available to carry out all this work makes up our energy supply.

The importance of fossil fuels

The world's chief sources of energy are, in order of importance, **fossil fuels**, water power and **nuclear energy**. Solar, wind, tidal, and **geothermal energy** also provide some of our energy needs. More than 85 per cent of the energy produced by businesses and governments comes from the fossil fuels (**petroleum**, coal and **natural gas**). These sources are called fossil fuels because they formed over millions of years from the fossilized remains of prehistoric plants and animals.

Petroleum: Petroleum supplies 40 per cent of the world's major usage of energy, mostly for transport and heating. Most petroleum is taken from deep underground, on land or beneath the seafloor, as a liquid called **crude oil**. Refineries process crude oil, breaking it down into kerosene, petrol (or gasoline) and other useful products.

A section of the Trans-Alaskan oil pipeline that runs over 1200 kilometres across Alaska.

Coal: Coal supplies over a quarter of the world's energy needs. It is used in the manufacture of steel, to drive steam engines and to generate electricity. In many parts of the world coal is used to heat people's homes.

Natural gas: Natural gas supplies 21 per cent of the world's energy needs. It is used to generate electricity, for heating and cooking and sometimes for lighting.

Once fossil fuels have been used they cannot be recycled or replaced and one day the supply will run out. Scientists and engineers are working to find ways of getting the most out of our fossil-fuel resources. They are also developing other sources of energy to replace them.

Problems to solve

Fossil fuels play a big part in our society but they bring many problems as well as benefits. Spills from oil tankers pollute coastlines. Burning fossil fuels releases carbon dioxide, a **greenhouse gas**, which many people believe is causing the Earth to warm up. Burning coal releases sulphur **compounds** that pollute the air. A great deal of effort is being put into the search for answers to these problems.

Coal provides the energy for the fierce heat needed to make steel in a blast furnace.

Photosynthesis

The process we have to thank for the **fossil fuels** that drive our cars and aircraft, heat our homes and cook our food is called **photosynthesis**.

Photosynthesis is the process by which green plants, algae and some bacteria capture the energy of sunlight and use it to make glucose (a simple sugar) from carbon dioxide and water. Photosynthesis is the source of nearly all of the energy used by life on Earth.

Chlorophyll

Photosynthesis takes place mainly inside the leaf **cells** of green plants. These cells contain a green pigment called chlorophyll, which gives the plant its green colour. Photosynthesis depends on the fact that chlorophyll can capture the energy of sunlight and use it to split water **molecules**.

Microscopic structures inside a plant cell allow it to capture the energy of the Sun.

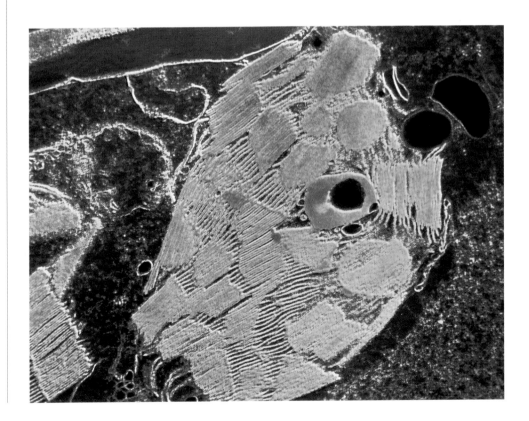

The chemical reactions involved in photosynthesis occur in two stages. First, sunlight is used to split water and, second, carbon dioxide is combined with parts of the water molecules to make glucose, a sugar. The process can be summarized by a simple formula:

carbon dioxide + water + sunlight = glucose + water + oxygen

Most of the glucose formed by photosynthesis is stored in the plant as starch. As animals eat the plant they also consume the energy that has been stored by the plant.

Photosynthesis is extremely important as it is virtually the only means by which energy (in the form of sunlight) can be made available for life. Without it, life on Earth would be limited to communities of organisms such as those that live off bacteria on the ocean floor.

A lucky benefit

Oxygen, which is given off during photosynthesis, is also of great importance to nearly all life, as it is needed to release energy from their food. Practically all the oxygen in the atmosphere has come from photosynthesis.

Every second the world's plants produce billions of tonnes of sugar using sunlight.

9

From forests to fossil fuel

Around 365 million years ago the first forests appeared on the Earth. These swampy forests were unlike any we know today. There were no trees, instead there were tree-sized club mosses and ferns, some with trunks over 30 metres tall. Much of what would one day be North America and Europe was covered in these fern forests.

Peat

There was not enough oxygen in the muddy forest pools for the **decomposers** that usually break down plant and animal remains to live. As a result, when the plants of the swamp forests died, they did not completely decay but were instead buried under layer upon layer of mud. As more plants died, this partly decomposed dead plant matter was compressed into a substance called **peat**. Peat still forms today where the conditions are right, and it is cut and dried for use as a fuel in many places.

Coal is formed over millions of years as ancient plant remains are compressed underground.

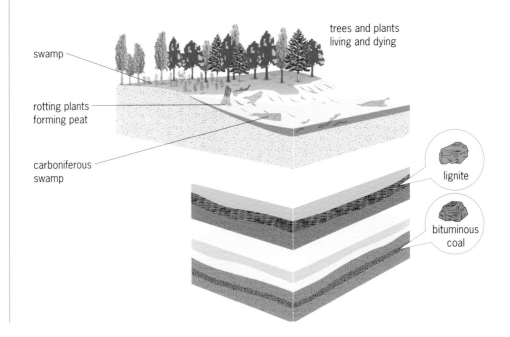

trees and plants living and dying

swamp

rotting plants forming peat

carboniferous swamp

lignite

bituminous coal

Coal formation

Over time, the peat deposits were buried under sand or other rocky materials. As these deposits built up, the pressure turned the deeper layers into rocks such as sandstone and shale. The weight of the rock layers pressing down on the peat began the process that changed it into coal.

A dark brown type of coal called **lignite** forms first. You can still see the plant material in lignite. As the pressure increases, the lignite turns into harder **bituminous coal**. Intense pressure at the deepest levels changes bituminous coal into **anthracite**, which is the hardest of all coals. Anthracites are the oldest coals and lignites are the youngest. Anthracites are over 300 million years old, whereas some lignites have formed from plants growing within the last million years or so.

Coal composition

Coal is chiefly composed of carbon, hydrogen, nitrogen, oxygen and sulphur, but the actual amounts of each can vary greatly. Coal is usually classed according to how much carbon it contains: anthracites contain about 98 per cent carbon whereas lignites have a carbon content as low as 30 per cent.

Samples of anthracite, the oldest and hardest of the coals.

Compact coal

Over two metres of compacted plant matter will eventually produce a seam of bituminous coal less than a third of a metre thick.

Sea-life energy

Petroleum, or **crude oil**, was formed from the remains of tiny plant and animal life-forms that lived in the world's oceans millions of years ago. As they died, their remains sank slowly through the water to settle in the mud on the ocean floor. Over a long period of time, this mixture of sand, silt and plant and animal remains got thicker. The process continues to happen.

As the deposits become deeper, the lower layers are affected by increasingly high temperatures and pressure. They are slowly squeezed to form **sedimentary rock**. The extreme conditions cause chemical changes in the **organic** remains. As a result, a waxy substance called kerogen is formed. At a temperature of around 100°C, kerogen separates into liquid oil and **natural gas**. At greater depths, where the temperature rises above 200°C, the bonds holding the **molecules** of the oil together begin to break apart. So, if the temperature is lower than 100°C little oil forms, if it is higher than 200°C the oil decomposes. This temperature range is called the oil window.

Oil can only be reached by drilling through the rock layers above it.

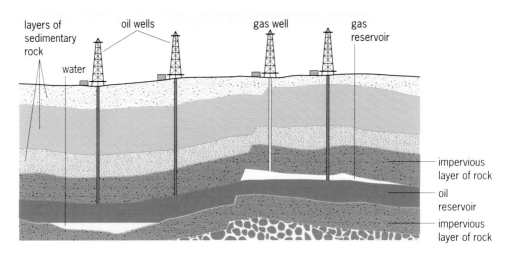

layers of sedimentary rock

oil wells

gas well

gas reservoir

water

impervious layer of rock

oil reservoir

impervious layer of rock

Pores and reservoirs

Sedimentary rock is filled with tiny cracks and holes, called pores. Oil and gas rise up through these pores. This may be a result of water in the rock pushing the oil upwards or because pressure from the rocks above squeezes the oil into the pores. Eventually, the oil and gas reach a layer of rock that they cannot pass through. They collect beneath it in a layer.

Some reservoirs form near the surface, but most are hidden deep underground. All oil reserves began beneath the seafloor, but over millions of years many places that were once ocean floors have become dry land. Sometimes oil reservoirs come to the surface and oil appears on the ground as **seepages** or springs. In Venezuela and Trinidad lakes of oil have collected at the surface.

A continuing process

Oil formation is still going on today beneath the ocean floor. However, it will take millions more years for the process to be complete, and we are still using oil much faster than it is being formed.

Oil rigs on Lake Maracaibo in Venezuela.

King coal

Coal is a useful fuel. The world's first coal industry was established in China by the fourth century AD. In many parts of Europe and Asia coal is still widely used for heating homes and other buildings. **Anthracites** are the cleanest-burning coals, and for this reason they are the best coals for heating homes. Unfortunately, anthracites are also the most expensive coals and so **bituminous coals** are often used instead to provide heating for factories and other large commercial buildings.

Native Americans in what is now British Columbia, Canada, burning coal for warmth.

Using coal

The amount of heat produced when a given amount of coal is burned is called its **heating value**. Bituminous coals are by far the most plentiful and the most widely used of the different types of coal. They have a slightly higher heating value than anthracites. Anthracites burn too slowly to be suitable for generating electricity, so bituminous coals are preferred. **Lignites** have a high-moisture content and are the least pure of the coals. They give a lot of smoke in comparison to the heat they give out. Coals with a low heating value, such as lignites, are rarely used for heating homes.

Coal and industry

Many substances are made from coal and then used as a raw material. **Coke**, for example, is made by heating bituminous coal to about 1100°C in an airtight oven. Keeping oxygen out prevents the coal from burning and the heat causes some of the impurities in the coal to boil off as gases. Coke is nearly pure carbon. Most coke is used in the manufacture of iron and steel.

Some of the gases produced during the coke-making process turn into liquid ammonia and **coal tar** as they cool. A light oil can be made from some of the other gases. Ammonia, coal tar and light oil are used to make drugs, dyes, fertilizers and other chemicals. Coal tar is also used for roofing and road surfacing. Coal gas is also produced in coking. It can be burnt like **natural gas** but gives off large amounts of soot.

Impurities

Coal is not a pure fuel – it has many impurities, one of which is sulphur. Coals that contain a lot of sulphur can cause serious air pollution. Some of the ash that is left behind when coal is burned may also escape into the air, adding to pollution problems. Filters are used to trap ash in **smokestacks** and prevent it from reaching the air.

A coking plant in Pennsylvania, USA.

Discovering petroleum

The word **petroleum** means 'rock oil' and people have been using oil from rocks for thousands of years. The ancient Egyptians coated mummies with pitch, a sticky black substance made from **coal tar**. Pitch was also used in the past to make wooden ships watertight. Native Americans used **crude oil** for fuel and to make medicine centuries before European settlers arrived in North America. In the eastern United States the remains of oil wells show that the Native Americans knew how to get oil from underground deposits.

In the mid-18th century, the American colonists found many oil **seepages** around New York, Pennsylvania and West Virginia. Some wells that were dug to mine salt produced oil, which was regarded as a nuisance. In the 1840s Abraham Gesner, a Canadian geologist, discovered kerosene. With the growing popularity of this fuel, which could be made from coal or oil, oil became more valuable.

Birth of the oil industry

In 1859 Edwin L Drake, a former railway conductor, drilled a well near Titusville, Pennsylvania. People called it 'Drake's Folly', not believing that he would find anything. However, Drake struck oil and soon other prospectors began to drill wells nearby. Within three years, so much oil was being produced that the price of a barrel fell from $20 to only 10 cents.

Edwin Drake's oil well at Titusville, Pennsylvania.

To begin with, wagons and river barges carried the oil to refineries, but soon railway lines had to be laid to the oilfields to transport the growing amounts of oil. In 1865, the first successful oil pipeline carried oil eight kilometres from Titusville to the nearest railway link. Within ten years, a 100-kilometre pipe took oil to Pittsburgh.

The industry grows

At first, kerosene was the chief product of the petroleum industry. Petrol, or gasoline, was seen as a useless by-product and simply dumped, often straight into rivers. This changed with the arrival of electric lights and cars at the beginning of the 20th century. Suddenly gasoline wasn't useless any more.

Supplies of petroleum were vital for the armed forces in the Second World War.

The First World War (1914–18) saw a huge increase in demand for petroleum fuels to power ships, trains, trucks and aircraft. After the war, more and more farmers in the United States and Europe began to use tractors and other oil-powered equipment on their farms. The Second World War brought another huge leap in the production of petroleum as more oil products were needed as fuels and lubricants. After the war the demand for petroleum kept on growing.

Natural gas

Natural gas is easily distributed through pipelines and can be used for a wide variety of purposes, such as heating and cooking in homes, schools and businesses. It can be quickly lit and just as quickly extinguished and can be burned in large or small amounts. Compared to coal and oil, natural gas produces much less pollution when burned.

Finding natural gas

Natural gas forms beneath the Earth's surface over millions of years as part of the same process that forms **petroleum**. This means that oil and natural gas are often found together in **porous** rocks such as limestone and sandstone. The gas cannot escape until a drill opens a hole through the surrounding solid rock.

Drilling for gas uses the same methods as those used in drilling for oil. Offshore gas wells are drilled in water as much as 2400 metres deep. Offshore drillers work from a barge, a movable rig or a fixed platform. Offshore drilling costs more than drilling on land but it is usually much more productive. Some of the richest offshore gas-producing areas are the Gulf Coast waters off the United States, and the North Sea around Europe.

A crew drilling for natural gas fit drill pipes together.

The gas industry

The natural gas industry began in the United States in the late-1920s when better pipes were made that could carry gas great distances economically. Up until the 1960s little natural gas was available in the UK. But, with the discovery of gas fields in the North Sea and in the former Soviet Union, natural gas use grew rapidly.

Explosive power

In 1967 a hydrogen bomb was exploded 1300 metres underground in northwestern New Mexico. The explosion allowed access to gas that had been trapped in rock formations that were too hard for normal drilling.

A drilling rig in the rich gas fields of the Gulf of Mexico.

Gas distribution

Natural gas is first taken to an extraction unit where impurities are removed. Next butane, propane and ethane are taken out at processing plants. The gas is then fed under high pressure into transmission pipelines, which can run for long distances underground.

Gas mains are large pipes connected to the transmission pipelines. Smaller pipes called service lines branch off from the mains, carrying the gas to homes, factories, schools and other buildings. Pure natural gas has no smell, so a chemical is added to make it smell so that gas leaks are more noticeable.

Working in a coal mine

Few jobs are more dangerous than that of the coal miner. Thousands of men, women and children have been killed in mine accidents and many thousands more have died of lung diseases as a result of breathing in coal dust. At one time, all mining was done by hand, using picks and bars. In the 19th century, when demand for coal was soaring, many miners worked underground for over ten hours a day, six days a week.

Children as young as ten wheeled the coal from the mines in the 19th century.

Modern methods

Today most mining work is carried out using machines. Miners don't spend so long underground and safety has been improved although there are still hazards. There are three main methods of reaching an underground coal **seam**. Where a seam is exposed, on the side of a hill or mountain, a mine can be dug directly into it. This is the easiest and least expensive method. The other ways are to dig an inclined opening or to excavate a vertical mine shaft through the surrounding rock to reach the coal seam. Once the seam has been reached a variety of methods are used to get the coal out.

In conventional mining, the coal is first cut using a large chainsaw on wheels called an undercutter. Explosives are then drilled into the coal to blast the coal from the seam. The coal is then taken in a shuttle car to a conveyor belt to be taken to the surface. Roof support is given by wooden timbers, steel beams set on posts, or steel rods anchored into holes in the roof.

The continuous mining system uses a single machine that does the job of the undercutter, drills, explosives and loading machine.

Strip mining

Strip mining, or surface mining, began in about 1910 when steam shovels were first being used. Today, 60 per cent of all coal is mined by this method. Often the coal is covered by soil, which must first be stripped off. The coal is then broken up with explosives.

Longwall mining involves extracting large blocks of coal, 100 to 200 metres in width. **Hydraulic jacks** provide roof support during the mining operations. These jacks advance as the coal is mined. The roof behind the jacks is allowed to collapse. The broken coal is removed to a conveyor belt for transport to the surface.

Even with modern equipment, mining is still hazardous.

Searching for oil

Before about 1900, oil prospectors drilled where they found an oil **seepage** and hoped for the best. Their equipment was little more than a pick and a shovel. Today oil exploration has become more of a science as **geologists** better understand how and why oil deposits are formed.

A nineteenth century engraving shows men being swamped by a gusher as Drake's Folly strikes oil.

Oil and geology

Oil geologists try to work out where oil might be found by studying rock formations. First, a detailed map of a promising area is made using photographs from satellites and aircraft, as well as from ground-level observations. The map is studied for signs of possible oil traps. For example, a low bulge might be caused by a **salt dome**, a common **petroleum** trap. The next stage is to take samples cut from layers of rock at the site. Scientists then look for signs of oil in the structure and chemical make-up of the samples.

Scientists can also locate structures that may contain oil with the aid of special instruments. The gravimeter, or **gravity** meter, measures the pull of gravity at a particular location. Different kinds of rocks have different effects on gravity. **Porous** rocks where oil might be found tend to give low readings on a gravimeter.

A magnetometer measures changes in the Earth's **magnetic field**. This is affected by the types of rock found beneath the surface. **Sedimentary rocks**, which may contain oil, often have weaker magnetic fields.

Seismographic surveys

The seismograph is one of the oil prospector's most valuable tools. It measures the speed of vibrations travelling through the Earth, either from an earthquake or from an underground explosion. The shape of many potential oil traps can be mapped by recording the changing speed of the vibrations as they travel through the rocks. A thumper truck is sometimes used to produce vibrations by striking the ground repeatedly with a large metal plate.

Seismographs allow geologists to look for fluids, such as oil or gas, in rock formations under the ground. Highly sensitive recorders are used to pick up changes in the height of the vibration waves as they are reflected from rocks that contain fluids. These variations appear as bright spots on the wave patterns recorded by the seismograph.

Thumper trucks being used in the search for oil in the desert of Libya.

Drilling for oil

No matter how careful a geological survey is, if oil is found, there is only one chance in fifty that there will be enough oil there to justify the cost of getting it out.

Preparing the site

A drilling site on land must be levelled and cleared. Roads have to be built and water and power supplies provided. After the site has been prepared, the oilrig is transported to the site. An oilrig is made up of drilling equipment and the framework to hold it, called a derrick. Once it is in place a construction crew will assemble it.

Rigging up

Setting up the oilrig is called rigging up. First, the crew erects the derrick over the spot where the well is to be drilled. Derricks range in height from 24 to 60 metres, depending on how deep the oil is believed to be. Hoisting machinery, to raise and lower the drill in and out of the well hole, is attached to the derrick.

Next, the engines that power the drill and other machinery are installed on the rig, along with a variety of pipes, tanks, pumps and other equipment. After the drill is attached to the hoisting machinery, the well hole can be started, or 'spudded in'.

Drilling

Cable-tool drilling involves using a steel cable to drop and raise a heavy cutting tool called a bit. Bits may be over 2 metres long and over 30 centimetres wide. Each time the bit drops, it cuts deeper into the earth. This method is used for digging shallow wells into hard rock.

Rotary drilling uses a bit attached to the end of a drill pipe. As the pipe is lowered into the ground it turns and the bit cuts into the rock. Different bits are used for hard and soft rocks. Extra lengths of pipe can be added as the hole gets deeper.

Drilling 'mud' is pumped down the pipe. It flows out of openings in the bit and back up the drill hole. The mud cools and cleans the bit and carries material from the drill hole to the surface.

Workers add piping to an oil well in Wyoming, USA.

Changing the bit

The bit is changed when it becomes blunt or if a different type of bit is needed. To change the bit, the crew must pull out the entire drill pipe, which may be more than 7.5 kilometres long!

Offshore operations

About a third of the world's oil comes from offshore oilfields. Offshore oil explorations are much more difficult than drilling on land. It can cost ten times more to set up an offshore rig than it does to construct one on land.

Drilling offshore

Drilling offshore involves taking the rig to sea. Wells drilled to explore a site are drilled from movable rigs, such as jack-up rigs and semisubmersible rigs, or on drillships.

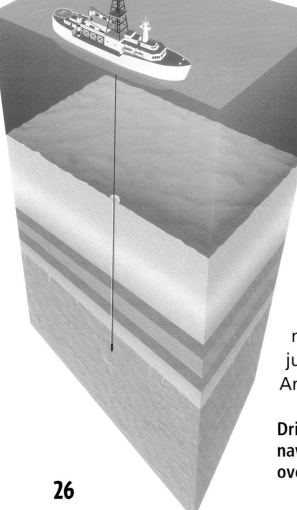

Jack-up rigs: These are generally used in depths of 60 to 100 metres of water. The jack-up rig sits on a floating platform attached to steel legs. When the rig is moved, the legs are jacked up off the seafloor, the platform is lowered into the water and boats tow it to a new site. Once in position, the legs are lowered and the platform is raised above the surface once more.

Semisubmersible rigs: These are used to search for oil in depths of up to 1200 metres. The rig is mounted on a **pontoon** suspended just beneath the surface of the water. Anchors keep the rig in position.

Drillships use satellite navigation to stay in place over a deep water wellsite.

Drillships: These are used in water up to 2400 metres deep. The derrick and other drilling equipment are mounted on the deck and the drill pipe is lowered through an opening in the bottom of the ship. Computers use readings from navigation satellites to keep the ship in a precise position over the drilling site.

Production platforms

Production platforms are only built and put in position after a reserve of oil large enough to justify the huge cost has been found. Most fixed platforms are used in shallow water, but they can be used in depths of 300 metres or more. The platforms are built in sections and taken to the drilling site in barges. The bottom section is guided into position on the seafloor using giant cranes. It is secured using giant stakes, called piles. A second segment can then be fitted on top. Some production platforms have three segments. The top segment is the base for the drilling operations.

An oil production platform in the North Sea burns off excess gas from the well.

Oil strike!

Drilling for oil is expensive. The crew of a rig want to know as soon as possible whether or not they will strike a good-sized oil reservoir. They look carefully for evidence of **petroleum** in the pieces of rock brought up in the drilling mud.

Riggers in China work to control a gushing oil well.

Testing for oil

Coring involves replacing the drill bit with a coring bit. This cuts out a sample of rock for analysis. Another test for oil involves lowering measuring instruments, called sondes, into the well hole. These transmit information about the composition, fluid content and other features of the rock.

Casing

If oil is found the riggers will reinforce the well hole with steel pipe called casing. The drill pipe is removed and the casing lowered into the well hole. Wet cement is pumped down the casing and covered with a plug that can be drilled through. Mud is pumped into the casing to push the plug to the bottom. The cement is forced up to the surface, filling the space between the well hole and the outside of the casing. Once the cement has hardened, the riggers can carry on drilling through the plug.

The casing acts as a protective lining for the well hole, helping to prevent leaks and the possible collapse of the hole. Also, at the top of the casing, the crew fits a giant valve, called a blowout preventer, that closes off the hole if pressure builds up in the well.

Coming into production

Bringing the well into production is carried out in several steps. First, an instrument called a perforator is lowered into the casing. When it reaches the depth where the oil has been found explosive charges are fired into the casing. The blasts punch holes into the casing so that the oil can enter. Next, the crew installs a string of smaller pipes that carry the oil to the surface.

Finally, a group of control valves is assembled at the top of the casing and tubing to control the flow of oil to the surface. Because of its many branch-like fittings this valve assembly is known as a 'Christmas tree'.

Valves for controlling the flow of lubricants to a North Sea oil rig.

Power stations

Life without electricity is hard to imagine. Electricity lights and heats our homes and provides power for computers, televisions, refrigerators, vacuum cleaners and a variety of other appliances. Machinery in factories, offices and hospitals also relies on electricity. Nearly all the electricity we use is produced by huge generators in power stations. Most of these power stations are burning **fossil fuels**, coal, oil or **natural gas**. Fossil-fuel power stations generate over 60 per cent of the world's electric power.

Superheated steam power

In the power stations the fuel is burned in a combustion chamber to produce heat, which is used to

An electricity **generator** inside a coal-burning power station.

boil water. The steam that is produced flows through a device called a superheater. The temperature and pressure of the steam in the superheater is raised by surrounding it with hot gases from the combustion chamber.

The superheated steam is used to drive a huge turbine, which consists of a series of wheels, each with many fanlike blades. As the steam flows through the turbine it pushes against the blades, causing the turbine shaft to

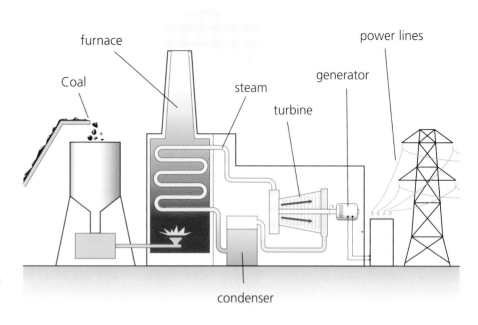

spin. The spinning shaft turns the rotor of an electricity generator, which causes an electric current to flow.

After the steam leaves the turbine it passes into a condenser where it flows around pipes of cool water. The heat from the steam is absorbed by the cool piped water and the steam condenses into liquid water again.

Spray ponds and cooling towers

The water that has absorbed heat from the steam has to be cooled before it can be used again. The heated water is pumped to a spray pond or cooling tower. At a spray pond, the water is sprayed out through nozzles so that it loses heat to the surrounding air. In a cooling tower the water spills down through a series of decks, cooling as it comes into contact with the air. The cooled water may be recycled through the condenser or simply discharged into a nearby lake or river, or into the sea.

Coal boils water to produce steam to spin a turbine to turn a generator to produce electricity.

Pollution problems

Fossil fuel power stations produce huge amounts of electrical energy but they also cause problems. Some release heated water into the environment, which may harm plant and animal life. The smoke from burning fossil fuels causes air pollution.

Moving the world

We depend on the internal combustion engine to make all the cars and trucks in the world move. These engines burn a mixture of fuel and air, turning **chemical energy** into **heat energy**. The heat energy is then turned into **mechanical energy** to perform useful work – making the car move.

Petrol engines

The most common type of internal combustion engine is the petrol-powered piston engine. Petrol engines are compact and light in weight in relation to the power they produce. Nearly all cars, motorcycles and tractors have petrol engines, as do many trucks, buses, aircraft and some boats. There are two main types of petrol engine, reciprocating (piston) engines and **rotary** engines. Reciprocating engines have pistons that move up and down or back and forth. A rod called a crankshaft converts this motion into rotary motion. A rotary engine uses rotors instead of pistons. The rotors produce rotary motion directly.

The four-step process by which an internal combustion engine works.

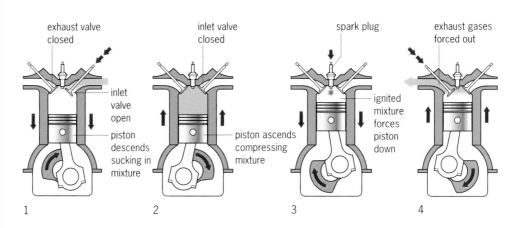

Car engines

Most car engines have several cylinders, each containing a piston and a spark plug. A mixture of air and petrol is forced into the cylinder and compressed. Then a spark from the spark plug explodes the petrol mix, sending the piston along the cylinder. The pistons are connected to a crankshaft. As a piston slides down the cylinder, it makes the crankshaft turn. The pistons are fired down the cylinders one after another and in this way the crankshaft is kept turning. The crankshaft is connected to the wheels of the car by a series of gears so that the wheels turn as the crankshaft turns.

Diesel engines

Diesel engines are mainly used for heavy-duty work, such as powering locomotives, freight trucks and buses, although some cars also use diesel engines. Diesel engines are heavier than petrol engines that produce the same amount of power but burn fuel oils which are cheaper to produce than petrol. The diesel engine compresses the air in the cylinders, causing the temperature of the air to rise. Fuel is then injected into the hot, compressed air and catches light. The explosion pushes pistons along cylinders to turn a crankshaft.

Near-death experience

The diesel engine was invented by Rudolf Diesel, a German engineer who built his first diesel engine in 1893. The engine exploded and almost killed him!

Diesel engines are often used to provide the power for large trucks.

Fossil-fuelled flight

Aircraft use two main types of engines: reciprocating engines (also called piston-engines) and jet engines, both of which use **fossil fuels**.

Piston power

Piston engines, are the most widely used type of aero-engine. Although they are not as powerful as jet engines they are still used for most light aircraft because they are more efficient at low speeds. An aircraft's piston engine is similar to one found in a car. They both burn a fine spray of petrol and air inside cylinders, driving pistons up and down to rotate a crankshaft. In an aircraft, the rotating crankshaft turns the propeller.

Engine power

The most powerful reciprocating engines ever used on an aircraft were the 2,722-kilowatt engines of the 1940s American B-36 bomber.

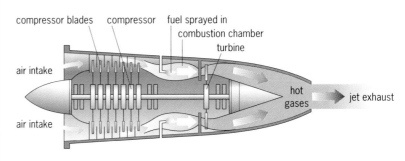

Cross-section through a jet engine.

Jet power

Jet propulsion works in the same way as air escaping from a balloon's neck, which makes the balloon fly around the room. As the air shoots out backwards, the balloon is thrust forward. Jet propulsion drives an aircraft engine in a similar way. Gas pressure inside the engine is produced by burning fuel in a combustion engine. (Most jet engines use a liquid petroleum fuel similar to kerosene.) The gases are directed out through a nozzle as a powerful stream of jet exhaust that pushes the engine forward.

Jet engines are much more powerful than piston engines even though they weigh less. There are three main types of jet engine: turbojets; turbofans, or fanjets; and turboprops.

Turbojet: A turbojet takes air in through the front and burns it with fuel to give a powerful jet of exhaust that thrusts the aircraft forward. The turbojet was the first successful jet engine and is still used today.

Turbofan: A turbofan has a fan at the front that draws in air. Part of the air sucked in by the fan is burned with the fuel and the rest is added to the exhaust, resulting in an exhaust that is much cooler than that of a turbojet, but at the same time more powerful. Turbofans are more efficient at low speeds, quieter and use less fuel than turbojets. Almost all new passenger jets have turbofan engines.

The fossil-fuel burning jet engine has radically changed world transport.

Turboprops: A turboprop is a combination of a turbojet and a propeller. It is basically a turbojet that uses its power to spin a turbine that turns a propeller. The combustion gases add a small amount of jet thrust to the propeller's thrust. Turboprops are much smaller and lighter than piston engines but produce the same amount of power.

Gas guzzlers!
A Boeing 747 uses a staggering 18 litres of fuel for every kilometre it flies!

The environmental impact

Removing **fossil fuels** from the earth damages the environment. Huge earth-moving machines gouge holes in the ground, sometimes many kilometres across, to get at coal **seams** in strip mining (see page 21). The waste materials, called spoils, tend to produce acids when they are exposed to rain. These may pollute nearby waterways as acid rainwater runs down the bare slopes, also washing away fertile soil.

Deep shaft mines produce waste material that is either dumped on the surface in huge tips or disposed of in the sea. Removing large seams of coal from under the ground can cause the layers of rock above to collapse, causing damage to buildings and roads and underground pipes and cables. Agriculture can also be affected as drainage systems are disrupted.

In the United States a great deal of controversy has been caused by oil exploration in the delicate **ecosystem** of the Arctic tundra. Leaks from wells drilled in shallow coastal waters and spills from tankers create oil slicks that pollute beaches and kill sea life.

The biggest mines in the world are opencast strip mines where minerals lie near the surface.

Oil spills

In December 1999 the 25-year-old tanker *Erika* broke in two, spilling more than 10,000 tonnes of fuel oil on French beaches.

In the United States, the Oil Pollution Act (OPA) came into force in 1990 after the *Exxon Valdez* oil spill caused huge environmental damage in Alaska. This legislation demands the use of double-hulled vessels, which are believed to reduce the chances of pollution in small collisions or groundings. In Europe, single-hull tankers above a certain weight will not be able to enter European ports after 1 January 2010, if proposed regulations become law.

Oil spills waiting to happen?

More than 2000 million tonnes of oil products were transported globally by sea in 1998.

Volunteers begin the difficult clean-up after an oil spill on the coast of France.

Air pollution and climate change

The major sources of air pollution are motor vehicles, factories and **fossil fuel** power stations. Air pollution **contaminates** the air with chemicals that can damage **ecosystems**, and are hazardous to health.

Many countries are working to reduce air pollution. For example, vehicles that are more fuel efficient and therefore burn less petrol are being developed. More power stations and factories are installing filters on their **smokestacks** to trap harmful chemicals from entering the atmosphere.

Trees damaged by acid rain in Poland.

Acid rain

Acid rain is caused by chemicals that are released into the air from vehicles and coal-burning power stations. These chemicals dissolve in water in the atmosphere to form sulphuric and nitric acids. Air currents can carry the acid many kilometres away from the source of the pollution before it falls in rain or snow, damaging crops, trees, lakes and buildings.

Many lakes in Scandinavia, the northeastern United States and Canada are so acidic that fish can no longer live there. Acid rain can also damage buildings and statues, corroding metal, stone and paint.

The greenhouse effect

Just as the glass in a greenhouse lets the Sun's rays pass through the glass but prevents **heat energy** from passing back out again, certain gases in the atmosphere prevent heat from the Earth's surface from radiating back out into space. This is why these gases are called **greenhouse gases**.

Carbon dioxide is a greenhouse gas that is present naturally in the atmosphere. However, burning fossil fuels produces carbon dioxide. About 7 billion tonnes of carbon dioxide are released annually. Natural processes, such as the absorption of carbon dioxide by trees, removes about half of this but the rest remains in the atmosphere.

Many scientists believe that rising levels of carbon dioxide and other greenhouse gases are causing the Earth's climate to become warmer. This effect is called global warming. The climate might become so warm that the sea level will rise as the polar ice-caps melt. Many coastal settlements will then be flooded. The effects of global warming could mean devastating floods and storms and changing weather patterns.

Heavy traffic in Mexico City. Cars are one of the worst causes of pollution.

Nonrenewable resources

As we have seen, the formation of **fossil fuels** takes many millions of years. This means that once our stocks of fossil fuels have been used up they will not be replaced in the foreseeable future. They are nonrenewable resources.

The world relies very heavily on fossil fuels and a great deal of effort will have to be made to find alternatives and use energy more efficiently. Ordinary people can help by being more energy conscious. If we use less electricity, less coal will have to be burned to produce it. If we walk or cycle instead of taking car journeys, less petrol will be consumed, pollution will be cut and resources will be saved.

Crisis? What crisis?

Between 1973 and 1998, world oil consumption rose by around 25 per cent to 26 billion barrels per year. At the same time, known oil reserves jumped more than 50 per cent to 1 trillion barrels.

One reason for this is a huge improvement in the technology used to find oil reserves. Three-dimensional computer-generated maps of underground formations mean that the chances of a discovery are improved. The development of drilling techniques has meant that more oil can be recovered from oil fields.

A technician uses a computer to analyse data that could help to pinpoint the location of an oilfield.

A horizontal drill can run along the length of an oil reservoir, allowing the oil to be removed more efficiently. Improvements in deep-water drilling techniques have allowed oil companies to drill in waters five times deeper than was possible a few years ago.

Energy alternatives

As fossil fuel reserves begin to run out scientists and engineers are exploring renewable energy sources. These include solar energy, wind, wave, and hydroelectric (water) power and **geothermal energy**.

Coal

Coal provides a quarter of the world's commercial energy needs. However, coal supplies are not under quite so much pressure as oil supplies. At current rates of production and use, the world's coal reserves should last for well over 200 years. Oil reserves on the other hand are expected to start running out in around 40 years.

China, for example, has colossal coal reserves. However, whereas most of these are in the northern provinces, demand for energy is growing fastest in the south. Because of the difficulty of transporting coal by land, China actually has to import about 50 million tonnes of coal a year. Australia is one of the world's largest exporters of high-quality coal.

A train carries a fresh supply of coal to a power station.

Fuel wars

Oil currently provides between 40 and 50 per cent of the world's energy needs. However, not every nation can produce enough to meet its own needs. Large-scale oil consumers such as France and Japan with no supplies of their own have always imported almost all their oil. During the 1970s, the United States changed from being self-sufficient in oil to having to import more than half of its oil supplies.

OPEC takes control

In 1960 the Organization of **Petroleum** Exporting Countries (OPEC), a group of the major oil-producing nations (not including Mexico, the United States and the USSR) was set up. The OPEC countries then began to take control of their own oil production from private oil companies. In the early 1970s, OPEC raised prices on **crude oil** to levels that affected the economies of all oil-importing countries.

Higher prices for petroleum-based fertilizers meant that the cost of food production rose. The developed world had less money to spend on importing goods from the developing countries since they were paying higher-prices for oil. At the same time, the developing nations had to pay more for imported goods because manufacturing costs rose.

Motorists tend to panic buy, making the situation worse, at the first sign of a fuel crisis.

A volatile situation

These effects on the world economy show how dependent we are on maintaining our supplies of energy. In 1998 oil prices dropped by about 50 per cent. This was because an economic crisis in Asia slowed demand, while a mild winter in the United States had the same effect. As a result, wells were shut down and exploration and drilling projects were postponed or stopped altogether in the United States. Around 65,000 jobs were lost in the American oil industry alone. Other oil-producing nations also suffered huge losses.

In March 1999, OPEC cut output by 1.7 million barrels a day. Four non-OPEC nations (Mexico, Russia, Norway and Oman) also agreed to cut their combined output by 400,000 barrels a day. Demand for oil improved as Asia recovered. The price of oil started to rise again.

Fuel alternatives

Japan is less dependent on oil supplies than it was in the 1970s. More than a third of Japan's electricity is now supplied by nuclear reactors, and industries such as software development, which use less oil, are growing.

The oilfields of Kuwait were devastated by retreating Iraqi troops at the end of the Gulf War in 1991. War can directly affect the price and availability of oil.

Fossil fuel statistics

World oil production

Countries with the largest proven crude oil reserves, 1996 (in millions of barrels)

Saudi Arabia	261,444
Iraq	112,000
United Arab Emirates	97,800
Kuwait	96,500
Iran	92,600

Countries with the greatest oil production, 1996 (in millions of barrels per day)

Saudi Arabia	8.1
Former Soviet Union	6.9
United States	6.5
Iran	3.6
China	3.2

- At the end of 1996, OPEC had proven reserves of 801,998 million barrels of **crude oil**. This amounts to 76.6 per cent of the world total.

- There are 11 members of the OPEC group: Algeria, Indonesia, Iran, Iraq, Kuwait, Libya, Nigeria, Qatar, Saudi Arabia, United Arab Emirates, Venezuela.

- The total world consumption of crude oil in 1996 was 71.7 million barrels per day (there are 159 litres in a barrel).

Natural gas production (in billion cubic metres per year)

Russia	640
United States	505
Canada	128
Netherlands	87

World energy production

Energy is measured in joules. A joule is a small unit so energy is usually measured in kilojoules (thousands of joules) or larger. In the following tables figures are given in terajoules (tJ), one terajoule is a million million joules.

Energy production, 1998

United States	76.6 million tJ
Russia	41.9 million tJ
China	39.5 million tJ
Saudi Arabia	21.5 million tJ
Canada	18.2 million tJ
Great Britain	12.1 million tJ

• The United States produces more energy and uses more energy than any other country in the world.

Energy consumption, 1998

United States	98.5 million tJ
China	39 million tJ
Russia	27.4 million tJ
Japan	22.6 million tJ
Germany	15.2 million tJ
Canada	12.9 million tJ
India	12.2 million tJ
Great Britain	10.6 million tJ

Glossary

acid rain   rain made acidic due to the presence of sulphur dioxide from coal burning, and nitrogen oxides from car exhausts and other sources. These gases dissolve in the water vapour in the air, forming sulphuric and nitric acids.

anthracite   hard, shiny type of coal that contains around 90 per cent carbon – its lack of impurities anthracite is less polluting than other coals

atoms   smallest units of matter that can take part in a chemical reaction, and the smallest parts of an element that can exist

bituminous coal   most common type of coal, which contains less carbon than anthracite and is the most often used solid fossil fuel

cells   smallest units of life capable of independent existence. All living things, with the exception of viruses, consist of one or more cells.

chemical energy   energy held in the bonds that hold atoms together in molecules. Chemical energy is released during a chemical reaction.

coal tar   a thick black sticky liquid produced by processing bituminous coal

coke   solid fuel made by heating coal in an airtight oven to remove impurities. Coke is around 90 per cent carbon and the most often used fuel in the iron and steel industries.

compound   chemical substance made up of two or more atoms of different elements bonded together

contaminate   to make impure by adding unwanted or undesirable substances

crude oil   see petroleum

decomposer   organisms that break down dead matter

diesel engine   type of internal combustion engine that uses the heat of highly compressed air to ignite a spray of fuel

ecosystem   community of living organisms together with their non-living environment

fossil fuels   fuels produced through the action of heat and pressure on the fossil remains of plants and animals that lived millions of years ago; the fossil fuels are coal, petroleum and natural gas

generator   a machine that produces electrical energy from mechanical energy

geologist   scientist who studies the origin, history and structure of the Earth

geothermal energy   energy extracted from hot rocks below the Earth's surface

greenhouse gas   gas in the atmosphere, such as carbon dioxide or water vapour, that absorbs heat radiated from the Earth's surface that would otherwise escape into space

gravity   the force of attraction between any two objects

heat energy   energy associated with the motion of atoms and molecules

heating value   measure of the amount of energy produced when a fuel is burned

hydraulic jacks   devices powered by water pressure and used for lifting heavy weights

Industrial Revolution   period around 1740–1850 when economic and social life in Britain and later the rest of the world was transformed by the introduction of coal-powered steam engines to drive machines for manufacturing. This meant that goods were produced in factories rather than a domestic setting.

internal combustion engine   engine in which the fuel is burned inside the engine

lignite   soft brown type of coal that contains about 50 per cent carbon

magnetic field   region around a magnet in which a force acts on another magnet or on a moving electric charge

mechanical energy   measurement of the amount of work that an object can do

micro-organisms   living organisms that are too small to be seen with the naked eye

molecules   two or more atoms joined together by chemical bonds

natural gas   a gas which contains mainly methane, but also some butane, propane and ethane. It can be refined and used for industrial and domestic energy.

nuclear energy   energy in the nucleus of an atom released when a large nucleus breaks down into two smaller nuclei (fission) or when two small nuclei combine to form a larger nucleus (fusion)

organic   describes something that comes from living or once-living organisms

peat   compacted plant remains that have partly decomposed in conditions of low oxygen

petroleum   thick yellowish black liquid mixture of hydrocarbons found beneath the surface of the Earth. It is formed by the action of bacteria and high pressure and temperature on the remains of plants and animals over millions of years.

photosynthesis   process by which green plants harness the energy of sunlight to make sugars from carbon dioxide and water

pontoon   a floating platform

porous   describes a solid that has many tiny holes or pores through which fluids can pass

rotary   relating to rotation or spinning

salt dome   underground structure formed when salt layers penetrate up through surrounding denser material in the Earth's crust. Petroleum is often found in association with salt domes.

sedimentary rock   rock formed over millions of years by the accumulation of layer upon layer of sediment deposited by wind, water or ice

seam   underground layer of a mineral such as coal

seepage   places where petroleum seeps out of the ground

smokestack   large industrial chimney

voltage   measurement of the force that moves an electric current arround a circuit

Index

Titles in the *Energy for life* series include:

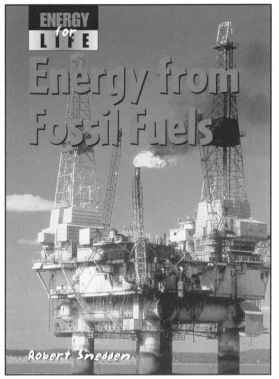

Hardback   0 431 14642 X

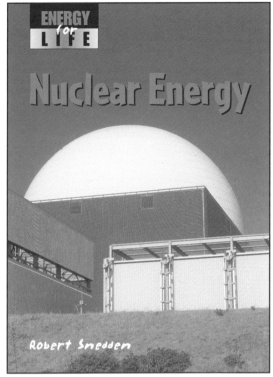

Hardback   0 431 14640 3

Hardback   0 431 14644 6

Hardback   0 431 14646 2

Find out about the other titles in this series on our website www.heinemann.co.uk/library